WHY IS THE SKY BLUE?

Questions & Answers About Nature

By Jack Long
Illustrated by Vern McKissack

Cover by Stuart Trotter

GALLERY BOOKS
An Imprint of W. H. Smith Publishers Inc.
112 Madison Avenue
New York City 10016

Why do cats purr?

Cats, from pet kittens to lions, purr to say "hello" or to show they are happy. A cat purrs by narrowing its voice box, or *larynx*. This disturbs the air flowing in and out of the cat's lungs as it breathes. The sound of the air going in and out is what we hear as a purr.

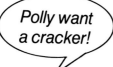

Polly want a cracker!

How do parrots talk?

Parrots do not really talk the same way people do. Parrots talk by imitating or repeating what you say to them. If you say the same word over and over again to a parrot, it will copy you. Once the parrot has learned a word it can say it whenever it wants to. Smart birds often pick up words on their own.

Why does a rattlesnake rattle?

A rattlesnake has loosely jointed rings at the end of its tail. When the snake wants to warn away its enemies it coils up and shakes its tail. The rings hitting each other make a rattling sound.

Why do grasshoppers hop?

Animals move in many different ways. They run, jump, crawl, fly, swim and hop. A grasshopper has strong back legs, which enable it to hop as far as twenty times its own body length. With its wings spread out, a grasshopper may glide even farther.

How does an earthworm crawl?

An earthworm is made up of many parts or segments. Each segment has its own muscles and two stiff bristles on the bottom which can grip the soil. To move, the worm stretches the front segments forward, making them longer and thinner. Then the worm pulls up the rear segments, making them shorter and fatter. The worm inches forward by stretching and shortening over and over again.

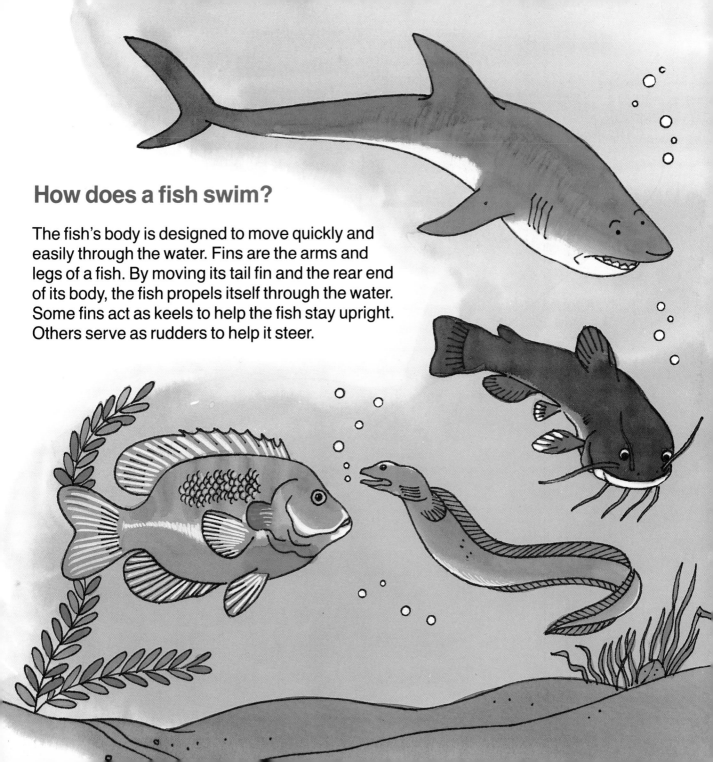

How does a fish swim?

The fish's body is designed to move quickly and easily through the water. Fins are the arms and legs of a fish. By moving its tail fin and the rear end of its body, the fish propels itself through the water. Some fins act as keels to help the fish stay upright. Others serve as rudders to help it steer.

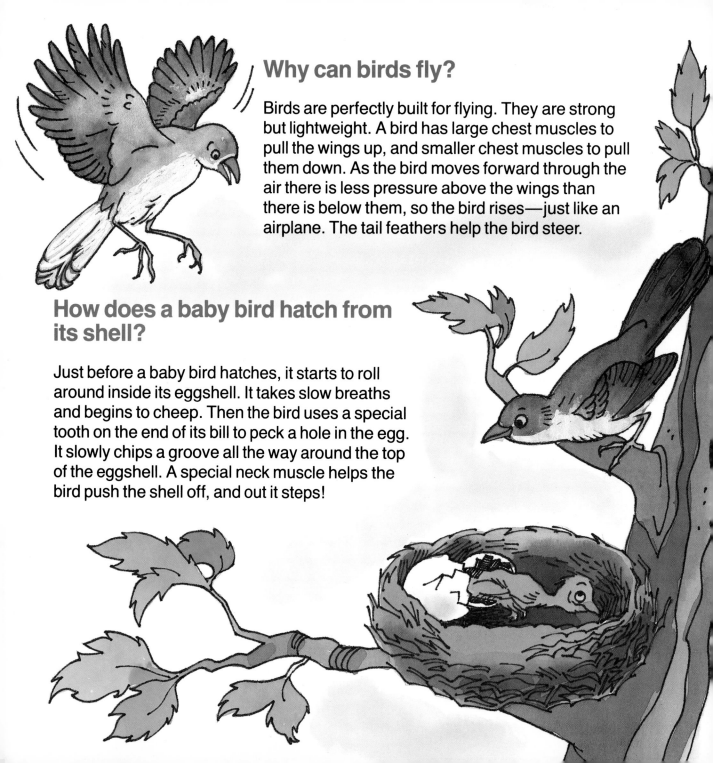

Why can birds fly?

Birds are perfectly built for flying. They are strong but lightweight. A bird has large chest muscles to pull the wings up, and smaller chest muscles to pull them down. As the bird moves forward through the air there is less pressure above the wings than there is below them, so the bird rises—just like an airplane. The tail feathers help the bird steer.

How does a baby bird hatch from its shell?

Just before a baby bird hatches, it starts to roll around inside its eggshell. It takes slow breaths and begins to cheep. Then the bird uses a special tooth on the end of its bill to peck a hole in the egg. It slowly chips a groove all the way around the top of the eggshell. A special neck muscle helps the bird push the shell off, and out it steps!

How do birds know when to migrate?

Many birds *migrate,* flying south every fall and north again every spring. Birds know it is time to migrate when the days get shorter, the weather gets cooler, and food becomes harder to find. In preparation for their long trip south, they eat large amounts of food to store fat. The migration instinct is so strong that some birds start their journey on almost the same date every year.

How do bees make honey?

A bee sips a sweet liquid called *nectar* from a flower, stores it in his body, and flies back to the hive which is made of honey-comb. The nectar is stored in a cell of the honeycomb. Other bees fan the cell with their wings to evaporate the water in the nectar. After about three days the nectar has become honey, which the bees seal with wax and store in the comb for winter.

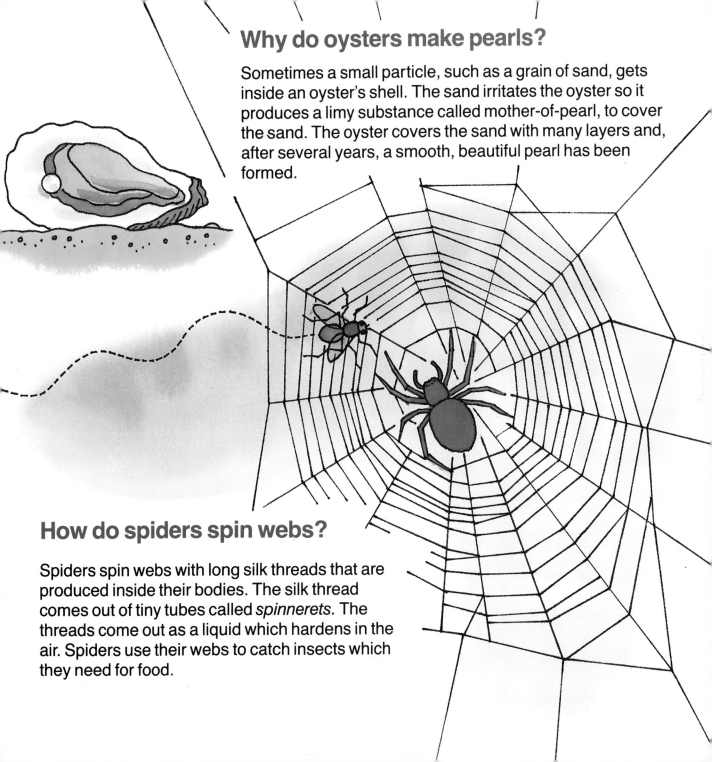

Why do oysters make pearls?

Sometimes a small particle, such as a grain of sand, gets inside an oyster's shell. The sand irritates the oyster so it produces a limy substance called mother-of-pearl, to cover the sand. The oyster covers the sand with many layers and, after several years, a smooth, beautiful pearl has been formed.

How do spiders spin webs?

Spiders spin webs with long silk threads that are produced inside their bodies. The silk thread comes out of tiny tubes called *spinnerets*. The threads come out as a liquid which hardens in the air. Spiders use their webs to catch insects which they need for food.

Why are there clouds in the sky?

As the sun warms the water on ponds, lakes, rivers and oceans, invisible drops of water, called *water vapor,* rise into the air. When the air carries the vapor higher into the sky, it cools. As the water vapor cools it changes, or *condenses,* into water droplets and ice crystals, which we see as a cloud. A cloud near the ground is fog.

Why does it rain?

The tiny water droplets in clouds bump into each other and combine to form bigger drops. As the drops grow larger, they become too heavy to stay in the air and fall as rain.

Why does it snow?

The water in clouds can behave in unusual ways. Sometimes, the water vapor in clouds freezes into tiny, tiny ice crystals. As more and more vapor freezes, the crystals grow into delicate snowflakes which fall to earth as snow.

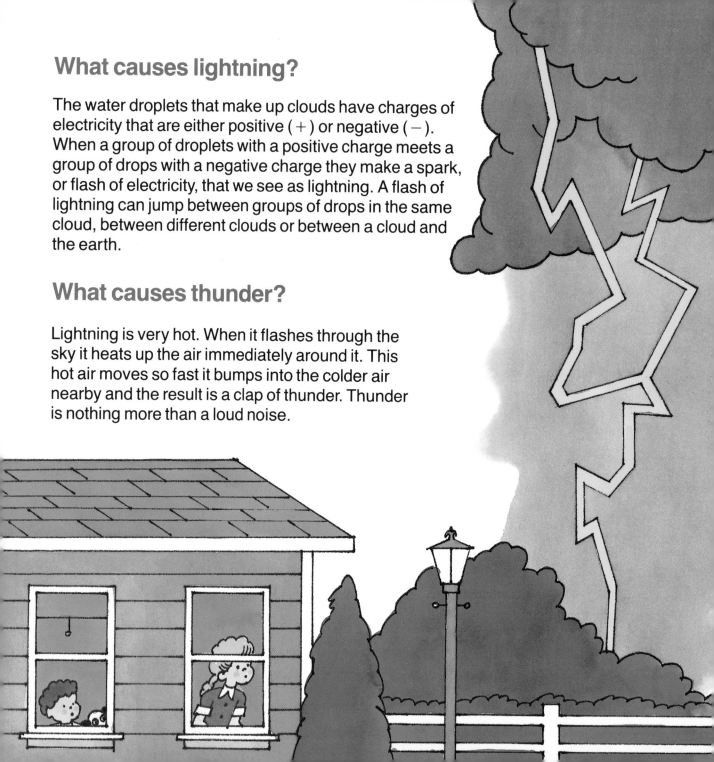

What causes lightning?

The water droplets that make up clouds have charges of electricity that are either positive (+) or negative (−). When a group of droplets with a positive charge meets a group of drops with a negative charge they make a spark, or flash of electricity, that we see as lightning. A flash of lightning can jump between groups of drops in the same cloud, between different clouds or between a cloud and the earth.

What causes thunder?

Lightning is very hot. When it flashes through the sky it heats up the air immediately around it. This hot air moves so fast it bumps into the colder air nearby and the result is a clap of thunder. Thunder is nothing more than a loud noise.

What is an iceberg?

An iceberg is a large mountain of ice that breaks off from a glacier and slides into the ocean. Glaciers are huge sheets of ice made from tons of snow that have been pressed together. Where the glacier meets the sea, the sea water softens the ice and giant sections break off and float away. Usually just the tip of the iceberg can be seen. The biggest part is underwater.

Why does the wind blow?

Energy from the sun warms the air around the earth, making it expand and rise. As the warm air rises, cooler air nearby moves in to take its place. This constantly moving air is wind. Wind is also affected by things on the earth's surface such as mountains, deserts and oceans.

What is a tornado?

Tornadoes are very strong windstorms that occur mostly in the central and southern United States in spring and early summer. A tornado is formed when warmer, lighter air from the south gets trapped below heavier, colder air from the north. In this stormy area, the warm air rushes upward and begins to spin. In this funnel-shaped thundercloud, wind speeds may reach 200 to 500 miles an hour.

What is fire?

Fire is the intense heat and light that comes from burning something. A fire needs three things to burn—fuel, like wood; oxygen from the air; and a temperature high enough to make the wood burst into flames. Fire is very important. It cooks our food, keeps us warm, and provides energy to run machines.

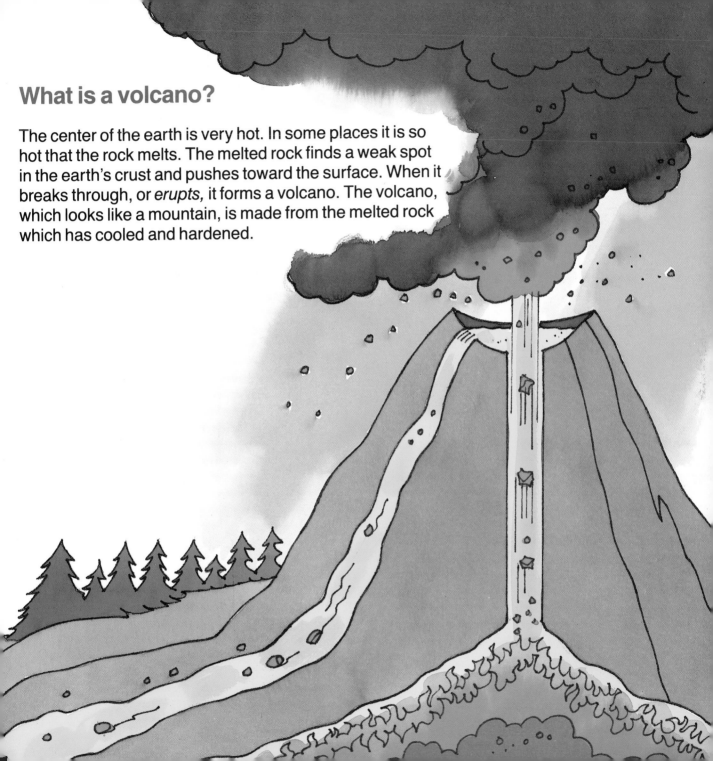

What is a volcano?

The center of the earth is very hot. In some places it is so hot that the rock melts. The melted rock finds a weak spot in the earth's crust and pushes toward the surface. When it breaks through, or *erupts,* it forms a volcano. The volcano, which looks like a mountain, is made from the melted rock which has cooled and hardened.

Why is there day and night?

Although you can't feel it, the earth is continually spinning.
Every day it makes one complete turn on its *axis*, an imaginary
line that runs from the North Pole to the South Pole.
When the part of the earth you live on faces the sun, it is
light outside. This is day. When that part of the earth turns
away from the sun it becomes dark. This is night.

DAY   NIGHT

Why are there different seasons?

At the same time that the earth is turning on its axis, it is also moving in a path around the sun. When the part of the earth you live on is closest to the sun it is warm and sunny. These seasons are spring and summer. When that part moves away from the sun the days become shorter and colder. This is fall and winter.

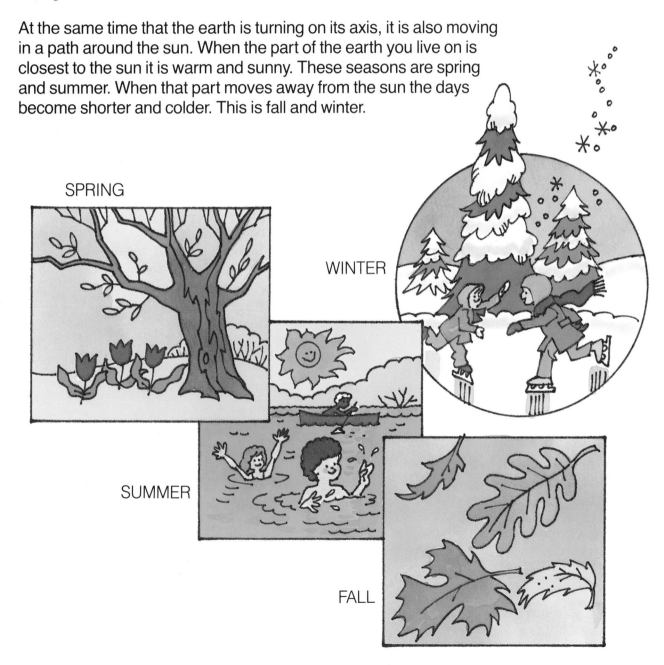

SPRING

WINTER

SUMMER

FALL

What is a desert?

Deserts are large, dry, sandy areas of the earth that receive little or no rain. One of the biggest deserts is the Sahara in Africa. Because of the Sahara's location, the air above it contains very little water. There are no clouds or rain. Deserts are so dry that very few kinds of plants and animals can live there. Camels are one of the few animals that can make the long trip across the desert without getting thirsty.

What is a jungle?

A jungle is a forest located in a warm climate where there is a lot of rain. The combination of warm weather and moisture makes a perfect place for all kinds of plants and trees to grow. Also called a rain forest, the jungle is home to many different animals, including tigers, monkeys, snakes, lizards, birds and butterflies.

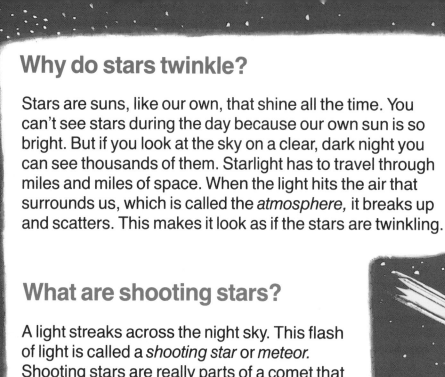

Why do stars twinkle?

Stars are suns, like our own, that shine all the time. You can't see stars during the day because our own sun is so bright. But if you look at the sky on a clear, dark night you can see thousands of them. Starlight has to travel through miles and miles of space. When the light hits the air that surrounds us, which is called the *atmosphere,* it breaks up and scatters. This makes it look as if the stars are twinkling.

What are shooting stars?

A light streaks across the night sky. This flash of light is called a *shooting star* or *meteor.* Shooting stars are really parts of a comet that have entered the earth's atmosphere traveling very fast. When they enter our atmosphere they heat up and glow, and then burn out.

Why does the moon change?

The moon travels around the earth just like the earth travels around the sun. The moon has no light of its own. What we see in the sky at night is the light from the sun reflected off the moon's surface. The moon seems to change size and shape because, as it travels, only a part of the sunlit half can be seen from the earth.

How are mountains formed?

Mountains are formed in many different ways. Most are made by movements of the earth's crust. Cracks, or *faults,* cause huge blocks of rock to tip up or drop down. In other places, underground pressures force the earth's crust into long lines of wavelike folds.

What causes earthquakes?

The earth's crust is made up of enormous, rocklike plates. Usually these plates fit together like pieces of a puzzle. Sometimes heat or other strong forces deep inside the earth cause the plates to move. When these huge plates move it makes the earth above shake.

How does a seed grow?

A seed contains a tiny plant with a small stem, a root, and leaves. The seed also contains a small amount of food to feed the plant as it begins to grow. Once it is planted in the soil, the seed needs light from the sun, moisture from the rain, and oxygen from the air in order to keep growing.

Why do plants need roots?

Roots anchor a plant in the ground and help it stand up. They reach into the soil for minerals and water, which the plant uses for food.

LEAVES

STEM

SEED

ROOTS

Why do flowers bloom?

Flowers bloom to make seeds that will grow into new plants. When a plant produces a flower, the bright colors and the pleasant smell attract insects, like bees and butterflies. The insects drink the flower's nectar. As they go from flower to flower, they carry the flower's *pollen,* or seed dust, with them. Flowers need pollen from other flowers to make seeds which will grow into new plants.

Why is grass green?

Grass, like other plants, is green because it contains a green coloring called *chlorophyll*. Chlorophyll helps plants change sunlight into food and energy. Because of the chlorophyll, plants like grass need only water and carbon dioxide from the air to make their own food.

Why do leaves change color in the fall?

Leaves really contain many colors. In spring and summer, we see mostly green because of all the chlorophyll that is working to make food for the plant. In the fall the leaf stops making food and the green chlorophyll disappears. Then we can see the other colors in the leaf, such as red, yellow, and gold.

Why is the ocean salty?

Even though the water in lakes, streams and rivers doesn't seem salty, there is salt in it. This water eventually empties into the ocean, carrying the salt along with it. When water evaporates from the surface of the ocean the salt stays behind. This has been going on for thousands of years so that now the water in the ocean is very salty. Swimming in the ocean is fun because the salt in the water helps you float.

Why is the sky blue?

The color of the sky depends on the atmosphere, the air above the earth. The atmosphere is made up of many gases such as *oxygen* and *carbon dioxide*. When the rays of the sun, which are made up of many different colors, shine through the atmosphere, they are separated and scattered. Blue light is scattered the most, so the sky appears blue on sunny days.

What makes a rainbow?

Sunlight is made up of seven different colors. When the light hits a drop of water, it is bent and split into its seven colors. If sunlight falls on many drops of water, usually right after it rains, the rays form an arch of the seven colors in the sky. This is a rainbow.

SUNLIGHT